Amelia Faces Her Anxiety

Question Guide

Tanya Popovski

Published by PoP-O Books 2018

Copyright © 2018 Tanya Popovski

www.popobooks.com.au

Copying of this book for educational purposes: All rights reserved. No part of this publication may be reproduced, stored in a retrieval system, or transmitted in any form or by any means, electronic, mechanical, photocopying, recording or otherwise, without the prior written permission from the publisher.

A catalogue record for this book is available from
the National Library of Australia.

Book cover design and formatting services by BookCoverCafe.com

First edition 2018

ISBN 978-0-6482019-1-5 (pbk)

Contents

Getting Started	1
Tips for Using the Question Guide	3
Comprehension Strategies	5
Title Page	6
Page Four	8
Page Five	10
Page Six	12
Page Seven	14
Page Eight	16
Page Nine	18
Page Ten	20
Page Eleven	22
Words and Phrases Used in Chronological Order	25

Getting Started

Kindergarten and year-1 reading expectations are quite different to those of mid to upper primary. In the early years, the focus is on decoding (learning how to read using symbols, sounds, sentences, and visual features). As the reader moves through the grades, the focus of reading in the classroom is about making meaning. The reader is then taught skills to deepen their understanding in order to read to learn.

The chosen book should be at a level below the reader's reading level. If you judge that the text is too difficult for the reader, choose a book at a lower level. This will allow the reader to concentrate on the meaning of the story, thereby encouraging higher-order thinking.

There is no need for pre-reading since a competent reader at this level will be able to read the text. The book should not be read in one sitting. Ask the comprehension questions after the reader has finished the text on each page. Continue to do this for approximately fifteen to twenty minutes. It is acceptable to take more than two sessions to complete questioning of the story. Go at the pace of the reader.

Tips for Using the Question Guide

The symbol ✪ indicates that an explanation for the word or phrase used can be found in the list at the back of this guide, which you can refer to for further clarification.

This book should not be seen as a text but rather a conversation of learning. When you have asked the reader each comprehension question, give them time to think before responding. The answers have been provided so you can give the reader the answer, which becomes a teachable moment.✪

If the reader has limited experience with a particular concept, take the opportunity to explore it further through the use of other resources (books, internet, etc). To use **Stop Annoying Me** as an example, if the reader has no understanding of the way a bull behaves, the words 'raging bull' will have no meaning. In this instance, you could take a moment to explain.

The answers provided in the **Question Guide** are general, and are given as examples only of acceptable answers. If the reader's answer is not relevant to the text, or cannot be justified with evidence from the text, this becomes a teachable moment. Give the answer, and show how you worked it out. The reader's responses do not have to cover all of the suggested answers.

If the reader's prediction of the title is not relevant to the clues on the page, avoid correcting their prediction straightaway. Instead, wait until they have finished reading the story to address the initial prediction. For example, you could say: 'At the beginning of the story, you predicted that the story would be [*repeat the reader's initial prediction*]. Now that you've read the story, how accurate do you think your prediction was? What clues could you have used on the title page to help you predict more accurately?'

The superscript numbers at the end of the questions relate to the tracking sheets (purchased separately at www.popobooks.com.au) and are linked to the Australian Curriculum.

Comprehension Strategies

Good learners draw on a range of comprehension strategies to deepen their understanding of written text. The *Question Guide* has been intentionally formulated to use the six comprehension strategies to explicitly teach how we understand texts. They are colour coded, with each colour corresponding to one of the six strategies.

Making connections Learners make connections with self, text and what is happening in the world.

Predicting Good readers use the information from illustrations, text and experiences to predict what will be read.

Questioning Good readers clarify meaning and aim for a deeper level of understanding by posing and answering questions.

Monitoring Good readers know what to do if something in the text doesn't make sense.

Visualising Good readers bring text to life by creating mental pictures from what they are reading.

Summarising Good readers are able to locate the most important ideas in a text and retell them in their own words.

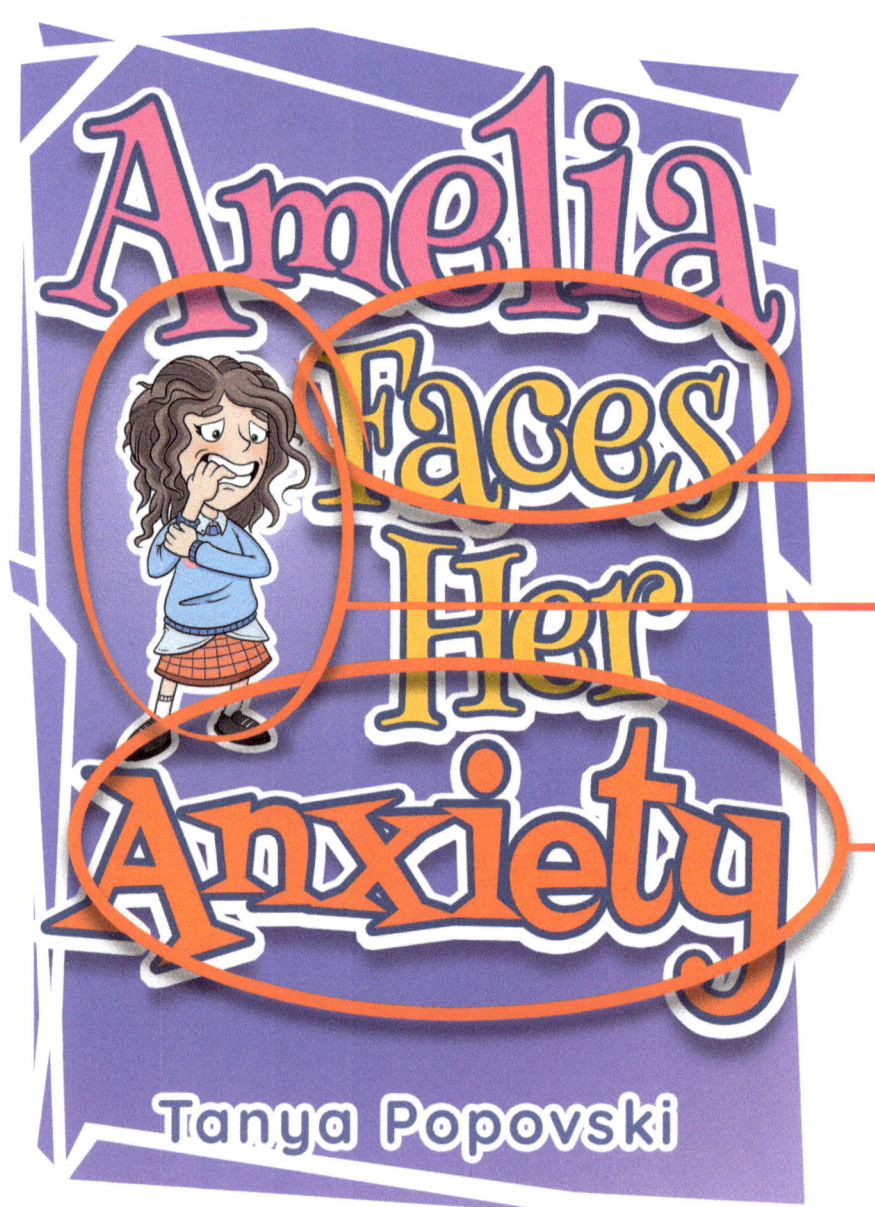

Title Page

Allow the reader to read the title and look at the illustration.

What do you think the story is about?[3]
The reader will respond based on the information on the front cover.

What is anxiety? Can you try to work it out from the context ⭐ (from within the sentence or part of the story in which the word is written)?[15]
Anxiety: a feeling of worry, nervousness or unease about an uncertain outcome

Can you replace the word 'anxiety' with another word?
Synonyms: worry, concern, apprehension, tense, stress

What does it mean to 'face' something?[12]
Face: to confront an issue, to deal with it

Is Amelia facing her anxiety figuratively ⭐ or literally ⭐?[12]
Figuratively, because Amelia's anxiety is an emotion and not something she can see or touch.
If the reader doesn't know the meaning of literal or figurative, use the explanation given in the list at the back of this guide. Once you have explained it, ask the question again.

What does the illustration tell you about the character, Amelia?[5]
She is a young, school-aged girl who looks worried.
If the reader gives a minimal response, you could use the following questions to prompt further analysis:
What emotion can you see on her face?
Does she go to school?
What is she wearing?

Can you remember a time when you felt anxious or stressed? Discuss.[1]
Reader to give a personal response

Amelia was worried. She read the school letter, and was scared and excited at the same time.

Year 5 was going on an overnight trip at the end of the year, with many fun activities planned for the two days. Amelia's friends were thrilled. Their eyes were alight with eagerness.

Page Four

Allow the reader to read the text aloud.

➤ What does it mean to be 'scared and excited at the same time'?[6]
Amelia was scared because it was an overnight trip, but she was also excited because she would be with her friends from her class.

Have you ever been on an overnight trip without your parents?[3]
Reader to give a personal response

How did you feel about the experience?
If the answer is no, ask:
How would you feel about being on an overnight trip without your parents?

➤ What does the word 'eagerness' mean?
Eagerness: excited and interested

What is this language describing: 'eyes alight with eagerness'? What is happening?[11]
When something exciting or good is about to happen, your eyes brighten.

Do you know how to skim and scan ⭐?
If the answer is no, use the explanation given in the list at the back of this guide.

Skim and scan ⭐ through the text to determine the main ideas ⭐.[16]
- Amelia was excited about the trip, but she was also worried about it.
- A lot of the children in the class showed excitement

Page Five

Allow the reader to study the illustration.

Look at the visual information the illustration is giving you. What additional information is shown?[7]
- The teacher is happy.
- Lots of children are happy reading the letter.
- A few children don't look as happy as the others.
- One boy is colouring in and not paying attention, so he may not know about the overnight trip.
- The children's eyes appear bright, indicating that they are eager. (Refer to previous discussion.)

How does this illustration help us to understand the story?
Most of the children are in a good mood: they are excited, happy, delighted. This helps us understand that the majority of the class are looking forward to the experience and are not worried.

In the playground, Amelia's friends were all talking about the overnight trip: who was sleeping in which room, what games and snacks they would take.

Amelia tried to sound happy and excited as well, but inside she was feeling very nervous. She had never stayed away from home before. She had never even slept at her grandparents' place. She couldn't go, but she didn't want to miss out on being with her friends.

Page Six

Allow the reader to read the text aloud.

What would you and your friends be talking about if you were going on an overnight trip? Would you talk about sleeping arrangements and what food to take? Why would you talk about games?[2]
Reader to give a personal response

Look at the text and identify descriptions of the way Amelia is feeling.[6]
'tried to sound happy and excited' (she wasn't really happy)
'inside she felt nervous' (she may have been feeling sick)
'she couldn't go' (she was feeling unsure and scared at the idea of being away from home)

Why is Amelia **trying** to sound happy?[8]
She didn't want her friends to know that she was worried/anxious.
She still wasn't sure if she was excited or scared.

Retell ✪ this part of the story.[17]
If the reader doesn't know how to retell, explain the process using the explanation in the list at the back of this guide.

- Amelia's friends were excited and talking about the excursion in the playground.
- Amelia realised that she had never stayed anywhere overnight and was feeling anxious about it. At the same time, she didn't want to miss out being with her friends.

Amelia decided that she wouldn't go. She just couldn't.

She talked to her parents about her feelings and how she felt about the whole situation. Her mum knew that this was going to be a lesson for Amelia in facing challenges, so she came up with an idea. They would practise for the overnight trip.

Page Seven

Allow the reader to read the text aloud.

➤ What is 'the whole situation'? What do these words refer to?[5]
Amelia told her mum that the class was going on an overnight stay and that she was worried about it. She felt that she couldn't go, but she didn't want to miss out on having fun with her friends.

➤ Why would Amelia's mum consider this a 'lesson'?[9]
Mum knew that there were going to be many times when Amelia felt anxious, and she wanted to teach Amelia that it's better for her to face the challenge instead of letting it beat her. Every time Amelia faced a challenge she would learn how to deal with it and it would get easier. If she let her anxiety stop her from doing things, she would miss out on much in the future; her anxiety would determine her actions.

➤ 'They would practise for the overnight trip': how would this practice help Amelia's anxiety?[8]
Practising would help Amelia feel comfortable about being away from her parents. It would help her get used to the idea.

If you were Amelia, how would you feel about the idea of practising for the overnight trip?[1]
Reader to give a personal response

Amelia and her parents agreed that Amelia should stay overnight at her grandparents' place a couple of times to get used to being away from home.

The first night was very hard for Amelia. She cried and wanted to change her mind about practising, but her grandparents spent time talking to her. They reminded her that the very next day she would see her parents again.

Page Eight

Allow the reader to read the text aloud.

▶ Why is there an apostrophe in the first instance of the word 'grandparents' but not in the second?[11]
grandparents' refers to the possessive; ✪
> **the home belongs to the grandparents**

grandparents refers to the plural; ✪
> **there are two grandparents**

▶ What did Amelia's grandparents remind her of?[5]
That she would see her parents the very next day.

Can you infer ✪ why it is important that she be reminded of that?[8]
It was important to calm Amelia when she started getting anxious. This helped her get past her fears in the moment and visualise the next day, when she would see her parents.

After her first practice night with her grandparents, it got easier every time, and when the day of the overnight trip arrived Amelia felt ready to face the new challenge. To her surprise, she felt a little excited, too.

Page Nine

Allow the reader to read the text aloud.

How many times do you think Amelia practised?[4]
Quite a few times: 'got easier every time'
More than once: 'after the first practice night'

Why was Amelia surprised that she felt excited?[8]
She had been anxious about the whole situation up to this point, so it was a big leap to go from anxiety to excitement.

Why do you think she was now feeling excited?[8]
She was becoming used to sleeping away from home and her parents, and because she wasn't so worried she could now look forward to the overnight trip.

How does the information in the illustration add to the story?[14]
It helps to show how Amelia is feeling; the reader gets a better sense of the mood she is in.

Amelia's overnight trip with her class was a success. She did feel anxious at times, but she was able to calm herself down by doing what she had done when she stayed with her grandparents. She just reminded herself that the very next day she would be home again.

Page Ten

Allow the reader to read the text out aloud.

➤ How did Amelia calm herself down?[4]
She thought about being home with her parents the next day.

Why do you think she thought about this?[5]
Her grandparents had kept reminding her about it, and it was true, the next day she went home and saw her parents again.

How would you describe Amelia's attitude (feeling) towards the overnight trip at this point?[13]
Overcoming the challenge of being on an overnight trip was worth it. She had the skills now to deal with being away overnight and she thought all the practice had been successful.
If the reader gives a minimal response, use the following questions to prompt further analysis.
- Before the practice, how was Amelia feeling? Was she looking forward to the overnight stay?
- After she overcame her fears and went on the overnight trip, how was she feeling?

Now re-ask the initial question: How would you describe Amelia's attitude (feeling) to the overnight trip at this point?

Amelia's parents were very proud of her. They knew she had learned the very important lesson of meeting challenges rather than avoiding them.

Page Eleven

Allow the reader to read the text aloud.

What was the lesson?[6]
To face a challenge and not avoid it.

Retell ⭐ the story in your own words.[17]
- Amelia read a school letter outlining an overnight trip.
- She didn't want to go, but she didn't want to miss out being with her friends.
- Her mum suggested that she face the challenge and prepare for the overnight trip by staying overnight with her grandparents over a period of time.
- During her stay with her grandparents, she learned to be calm and think about the end result.
- She was able to go to the overnight trip and use her new skills to help her face her challenge.
- Her parents were very proud of her for facing this challenge.

Can you infer what might have happened if she had avoided going on the overnight trip?[8]
- She would have missed out on having fun with her friends.
- Her friends would have talked about the overnight trip when they got back, and she would have felt left out because she hadn't had the same experience.
- She wouldn't have learned to face her anxiety, or use her new skills in other situations.

What generalisations ⭐ can you make about the story?[18]
- Facing a challenge requires taking action.
- Practise doing something that you have a fear of and it will get easier.
- Always talk to an adult you trust if something is worrying you.

Words and Phrases Used in Chronological Order

teachable moment An unplanned opportunity that arises in the classroom where the teacher has an ideal chance to offer insight to their students; not something that can be planned for; a fleeting opportunity that must be sensed and seized by the teacher. If the reader is unable to answer the question, answers the question incorrectly, or after prompting is still unsure, take the opportunity to tell them the answer and show them how you reached that conclusion.

literal Taking words in their usual or most basic sense without metaphor or exaggeration.

figurative A meaning that is different from the basic meaning, expressing an idea in an interesting way by using language that describes something else
(e.g. *It's raining cats and dogs*. This is a figurative description of heavy rain; if the meaning were literal, cats and dogs would be falling from the sky).

exaggeration Magnification beyond the limits of truth; to overstate or represent disproportionately.

metaphor A figure of speech in which a word or phrase is applied to an object or action to which it is not literally applicable.

skim and scan To skim is to read text very quickly; to scan is to locate specific pieces of information in the text without having to read each individual word.

retell To determine what is important; to retell a story in sequence, and with the correct facts.

possessive A noun indicating ownership
   (e.g. *The dog's bed*).
plural An amount greater than one
   (e.g. *Ten apples*).
infer When you use clues from the story to figure out something that the author doesn't tell you. Using facts, observations and reasoning to come up with an assumption or conclusion
   (e.g. *The ground was wet and the leaves were moving around.* Inference: It had been raining and it was windy.
   On Jocelyn's return from her holiday, her plants were limp and droopy. Inference: Her plants had not been watered during the time that she was away.)
generalisation A broad statement that applies to many examples, formed from several examples or facts in a story. Find the most important ideas in the story and justify (prove) your answer.
context The words, sentences, and ideas that come before and after a word or phrase.
main ideas Teaching readers to know what the main ideas are can be difficult. The main idea is the most important part of the story. It helps readers to understand what the story is mainly about without too much detail. Think of who and what to generate the main ideas.

Learn with

www.ingramcontent.com/pod-product-compliance
Lightning Source LLC
Chambersburg PA
CBHW062107290426
44110CB00022B/2736